GUIDE TO GHOSTS AND HAUNTINGS

Ghosts

Doreen Staskal

San Diego, CA

© 2025 ReferencePoint Press, Inc.
Printed in the United States

For more information, contact:
ReferencePoint Press, Inc.
PO Box 27779
San Diego, CA 92198
www.ReferencePointPress.com

ALL RIGHTS RESERVED.
No part of this work covered by the copyright hereon may be reproduced or used in any form or by any means—graphic, electronic, or mechanical, including photocopying, recording, taping, web distribution, or information storage retrieval systems—without the written permission of the publisher.

LIBRARY OF CONGRESS CATALOGING-IN-PUBLICATION DATA

Names: Staskal, Doreen, author
Ghosts/by Doreen Staskal
Series: Guide to Ghosts and Hauntings
Description: San Diego, CA : ReferencePoint Press, Inc., 2025. | Includes bibliographical references and index.
 Identifiers: LCCN 2024043946 (print) | ISBN 978-1-6782-0992-6
 (library binding) | ISBN 978-1-6782-0993-3 (ebook)

CONTENTS

**Spirits and the Spirit World:
What People Believe** — 4

Introduction — 5
The Enduring Fascination with Ghostly Encounters

Chapter One — 8
What Are Ghosts, and Why Do They Appear?

Chapter Two — 18
Making Themselves Known

Chapter Three — 28
How Do They Do It?

Chapter Four — 37
Ghosts of Many Cultures

Chapter Five — 46
Science Explains Ghosts

Source Notes — 57
For Further Research — 59
Index — 61
Picture Credits — 64
About the Author — 64

SPIRITS AND THE SPIRIT WORLD: WHAT PEOPLE BELIEVE

Belief in Spirits

% of US adults who say . . .

They believe people have a soul or spirit in addition to their physical body	83%
There is something spiritual beyond the natural world, even if we cannot see it	81%
There are some things that science cannot possibly explain	74%
They have had a sudden feeling of connection with something from beyond this world	45%
They have a strong feeling that someone who has passed away was communicating with them from beyond this world	38%
They believe spirits or unseen spiritual forces exist and they have personally encountered one	30%

Communication Between the Living and the Dead

% of US adults who believe it is definitely or probably true that people who have died can . . .

Be united with other loved ones who have already died	57%
Provide assistance, protection, or guidance to the living	46%
Be aware of things going on among the living	44%
Communicate with the living	42%
Be reincarnated	27%
Harm the living	18%

Hearing from the World Beyond

% of US adults who say they . . .

Have had a sudden feeling of connection with someone from beyond this world	45%
Have had a strong feeling that someone who has passed away was communicating with them from beyond this world	38%
Believe spirits or unseen spiritual forces exist and they have personally encountered one	30%

INTRODUCTION

The Enduring Fascination with Ghostly Encounters

Jacqueline visited her grandmother's house often when she was a little girl. Her great-grandparents, Grannie June and Pa Hank, lived there, too. Jacqueline loved sitting under a tree in their backyard making daisy chains. Pa Hank would often sit with her and tell her stories. Many were about his life, and Jacqueline found them interesting. Sometimes he talked about Prohibition, a period in US history when alcohol was outlawed.

As an adult, Jacqueline had fond memories of sitting with her great-grandfather. There was just one problem: Jacqueline was born in 1982, and Pa Hank had died in 1981.

When little Jacqueline would tell her family about her conversations with Pa Hank, they did not seem overly concerned. She later realized that this was probably because they all believed his spirit regularly visited the home. Grannie June said she frequently saw angels in the yard and often talked with the deceased Hank. The rest of the family also felt he was nearby. They heard cupboard doors opening and closing in the early mornings and attributed the noises to Hank going about his usual morning routine.

Once grown, Jacqueline knew that logically she could not have been sitting with Pa Hank. She also knew that, without a doubt, she had done so. The man in the yard was completely real to her—as real as anyone else she spoke with every day. As she noted, "It never felt like ghosts, it felt like talking to my Pa Hank."[1]

Jacqueline knew that others would find her experience unbelievable. But if she were not communicating with Pa Hank, she wondered how her six-year-old self could know about Prohibition—a time that took place sixty years before she was born.

A Common Belief

Jacqueline was so sure she had spent time with the spirit of her great-grandfather that she described her experiences on a podcast in which people share supernatural encounters. The show's creator, Derek Hayes, says he developed the show to give people like Jacqueline a place to talk through their strange experiences.

Hayes receives hundreds of calls every week from people all over the world. Although he finds logical explanations for much of what he is told, some stories leave him completely baffled. And frightened. He is especially affected by personal stories like Jacqueline's. According to Hayes, "Every once in a while, somebody will call in one of those personal [ghost] stories. It's that personal connection for me that really brings it home. And some of those are just terrifying."[2]

> "Every once in a while, somebody will call in one of those personal [ghost] stories. It's that personal connection for me that really brings it home. And some of those are just terrifying."[2]
>
> —Derek Hayes, creator and host of *Monsters Among Us* podcast

It is not just these podcast listeners who believe in ghosts. The belief is, in fact, quite common. One recent survey found that 61 percent of the US population believes that ghosts are real. For many this goes beyond a simple belief in their existence. One in every five people say they have personally encountered a supernatural entity. That amounts to more than 50 million people who believe they have met some sort of ghost.

Reflections in Pop Culture

American popular culture reflects a keen interest in the topic. Movies about ghosts—such as *The Amityville Horror*, *Field of Dreams*,

Research shows that a large percentage of people believe that ghosts are real.

The Sixth Sense, *Ghostbusters*, and *The Shining*—have become classics. Television shows about ghosts abound, ranging from comedies to dramas to reality shows. And thousands of fiction and nonfiction books about ghosts are sold every year.

There has also been a profusion of podcasts about ghosts in the past ten years. Many, like Hayes's, are forums for those who want to tell about their personal experiences with spirits. These podcasts seem to have a never-ending supply of stories as well as loyal audiences. Other podcasts interview people who research ghosts. These shows have also attracted many followers.

Additionally, people seem eager to have a personal encounter with ghosts. The internet is full of sites that sell ghost-hunting equipment. Ghost tours of buildings, neighborhoods, cemeteries, and other purportedly haunted places are frequently fully booked with the curious. During these tours, people hear stories about the resident ghosts and their earthly lives. Occasionally, guests believe they experience an unearthly entity.

And of course, no slumber party or campfire is complete without at least one ghost story. Some stories are classics that have been around for years. Others are personal stories the tellers swear happened to them. Indeed, the popularity of the question "Are ghosts real?" never seems to die.

What Are Ghosts, and Why Do They Appear?

People have reported seeing ghosts for centuries, but agreeing on just what these apparitions are and why they appear is difficult. In general, people think of ghosts as beings who belong to other worlds or realms yet occasionally visit the earth. Some ghosts are believed to be nonhuman entities that are attracted to the living. Certain religions, for example, believe in demon ghosts that seek to wreak havoc on a person's life. However, most ghosts are thought to be the spirits of deceased humans who haunt people or places with which they are associated. Therefore, many people who are intrigued by ghosts assume these souls act and sometimes think and communicate as their former selves would.

Spirits Who Do Not Move On

Mediums are people who believe they can communicate with spirits of the dead. Kerrie Erwin is a medium who thinks that most ghosts are earthbound because they have not yet moved on from their earthly lives. She says that although many people do not see them, these spirits are all around. "Earthbound spirits are literally everywhere, and can be seen or felt by sensitive souls and mediums that have abilities."[3]

According to Erwin, there are several reasons earthbound spirits do not move on to an afterlife or eternal rest. One is because they do not want to. They may have unfinished business or a great attachment to a person, object, or location. Some spirits do not know how to move on. Others do not move on because they do not yet understand that they are dead.

A woman named Julie believes she met this kind of spirit one day as she drove by a terrible car accident. As she passed the wreckage, a woman suddenly appeared in her passenger seat. Both Julie and the woman were startled and upset. Julie quickly surmised that the woman's appearance was somehow connected to the accident. She told the woman, "Ma'am, you need to calm down, my name is Julie and I'm here to help."[4] She then encouraged her to move into the sunshine outside. At this point, the woman drifted out of the car and into the distance. Julie had managed to keep her cool during the experience, but afterward she was shaken.

Several days later Julie was watching television when a story about the crash came on the news. A picture of the woman who had died in the accident appeared on the screen. Julie was shocked. It was a picture of the very same woman who had been in her car the day of the accident.

Ghosts Who Comfort

One psychic medium who goes only by Kate says she has seen and communicated with spirits since she was a young child. She says that spirits often appear to assure family and friends that they are still around and watching over them. When speaking of the spirits of deceased loved ones, she says, "What I have learned the most about this world is that for the most part, the main message everybody wants to get across is a message of love and

> "Earthbound spirits are literally everywhere, and can be seen or felt by sensitive souls and mediums that have abilities."[3]
>
> —Kerrie Erwin, medium

A medium is a person who believes that they can communicate with spirits of the dead.

safety. I think that love is the basis for everything . . . most of the time [spirits] are coming in to say hey I love you."[5]

Author Bill Guggenheim came to the same conclusion after years of study. He was once a stockbroker who had never believed in life after death. He had always thought that "when you're dead, you're dead."[6]

But then he started receiving messages from people who had already died, some from people he did not know. These would be in the form of thoughts or some kind of writing. The spirits would ask him to give messages to their living loved ones. Guggenheim began questioning his sanity.

To find answers, he embarked on a study of religions and spirituality. From it he learned about a phenomenon he came to call after-death communication (ADC). An ADC is a message from a person who has already passed. The communication might come as a touch, dream, vision, or even telephone call.

Guggenheim and his wife started collecting stories of ADCs and eventually amassed over three thousand. As a result, Guggenheim says he became convinced that "receiving a message from a loved one who has died is as common as receiving a greeting card from someone who is living."[7] Though he formerly scoffed at ghosts, Guggenheim came to believe that a person's soul survived death and could visit the living world.

A man named Josh believes he had an ADC when he was twelve years old. At the time, Josh was very close to his grandfather. When his grandfather was diagnosed with cancer, Josh spent as much time with him as he could. One night after visiting him, Josh woke up around 2:00 a.m. to see his grandfather standing next to him.

Josh stared at his grandfather and heard him say, "Everything will be OK."[8] Then his grandfather walked away. Josh got up to follow him, but he turned when the phone in another room rang. Josh heard his aunt answer it and looked back toward his grandfather. The older man was gone. A moment later the aunt came into the room crying. She told Josh that his grandfather had just died.

This kind of experience does not surprise psychic Karen Noe. She says she believes that "our deceased loved ones often come around us to let us know they are okay. When they do, they retain their original personality, one of the ways to tell messages are from them."[9]

> "Our deceased loved ones often come around us to let us know they are okay. When they do, they retain their original personality, one of the ways to tell messages are from them."[9]
>
> —Karen Noe, psychic

Loved Ones Who Come to Help

More than half of all US adults say they have been visited by the spirit of a deceased loved one. Author and medium Claire Broad says that visits from the dead are indeed real. She herself has had them for as long as can remember. Broad says we are all spiritual beings who can connect with other spiritual beings, even if they are deceased. According to Broad, spirits come to tell people that they are not alone, and they often appear just when a person needs them the most.

Third Man Factor

The "third man factor" is the name given to an experience in which an unknown spirit helps a person in crisis. Ron DiFrancesco experienced this kind of help when on September 11, 2001, hijacked planes crashed into the World Trade Center building, where he worked. Panicked, he immediately headed toward the stairs.

As DiFrancesco started down the steps, he met people coming up. They told him that the way down was blocked by fires and debris. They were trying to escape by going up. DiFrancesco started to follow them. But then he heard a voice tell him to go down, not up. He had no idea who had said this, and going down seemed like a bad idea. Yet DiFrancesco felt compelled to follow the advice.

Wreckage blocked the stairwell, but DiFrancesco pushed his way through, feeling guided by a presence. Finally, he reached ground level and staggered outside. Minutes later the building collapsed, and DiFrancesco was knocked unconscious. He woke up in a hospital injured but alive.

DiFrancesco later learned he was the last person to make it out of the building. No one going up had survived. He attributed his survival to the unknown presence that had guided him.

Eilish Poe believes she had deceased loved ones come to her in a time of dire need. Shortly after Poe broke up with her boyfriend, he came to her home and attacked her with a knife. After he stabbed her several times, Poe decided to play dead, hoping this would make him leave. It did.

Poe was losing lots of blood and needed help fast. But she could not find her phone and was ready to give up. Then a strange thing happened. Poe's grandmother appeared in front of her—a woman who had died years earlier. Her grandmother was not talking, she was just standing and smiling at Poe. Poe found the vision comforting. Then her grandmother faded away and was replaced by Poe's best friend from high school. She, too, was dead. Like Poe's grandmother, the friend just stood there smiling. Poe was again comforted.

Next, the friend faded away and a woman named Alyssa Burkett appeared. Poe knew that Burkett had been murdered by an ex-boyfriend. "She was there for a reason," Poe says. "She was there to get me out of there." Poe watched as Burkett "pushed the air" at Poe with her hands, leaving her with renewed energy. "The next thing I know," says Poe, "she literally pulled me up, and I was sitting upright, and I hadn't been sitting upright on my own, the entire time."[10]

Poe felt new hope. She started looking for her phone again and finally found it. She tried tapping 911. Her fingers were so wet with blood, though, that the screen did not respond. She then used her knuckles to push the volume and lock buttons to bring up the emergency screen. But once more her blood-covered fingers would not swipe the screen. As a last resort, Poe bent over and used the tip of her nose to slide the command. It worked. The 911 operator answered, and emergency services arrived within minutes.

Poe spent many months recovering. But she lived. She attributes her survival to the three ghosts who appeared to her. Poe later said that seeing these beings in her moment of peril made her "feel like people and souls are out there for us in ways that we don't understand."[11]

Some people say that they have been visited by the spirit of a deceased loved one who came to help them in a time of need.

Guardian Ghosts

It is not always loved ones who act as helpful spirits. According to author Tanya Carroll Richardson, "No matter who you are, where you come from, or what your life looks like, you have spirit guides sending you helpful messages."[12] Richardson says that some spirits watch over the same person all the time. Others appear to people only in specific situations.

Indeed, people have reported being rescued by unknown entities. Frequently, these guardians appear and disappear with no one else having seen them.

Medium Ivory LaNoue tells of a woman who was in terrible pain after a surgery. One night she woke up at 2:45 a.m. in her hospital room to find a woman in a white uniform sitting on her bed reading aloud from the Bible. When the woman asked the visitor who she was, the visitor replied, "I was sent here to make sure you'd be alright. You are going to be fine. Now you should get some rest and go back to sleep."[13] In the morning the woman asked hospital staff who had visited her. She was told that no one had been there that night.

Demons

Kerrie Erwin says that not all ghosts are loving and helpful. Some beings' purpose is to bring humans strife. Many people call these beings demons. Occult expert Michelle Belanger defines a demon as a nonhuman entity that has intelligence and malevolent intent. According to Belanger, the purpose of demons is to bring disharmony and unhappiness to the people they visit. She says that demons are smart, cunning, old, and patient. Belanger believes that true demons are rare but do exist.

Many religions believe that demons are part of an eternal battle between good and evil. Christians believe that demons work for the devil and that their goal is to gain possession of a human soul and turn a person away from God. Demons can disguise themselves as an acquaintance or a loved one to gain the confi-

Crime-Solving Ghosts?

Some ghosts, like Teresita Basa, may return to the living world to seek justice. In 1977 Basa was stabbed to death in her home. The police found no suspects. They eventually stopped investigating and marked the case as unsolved.

Sometime after the case was closed, a doctor came to the police to tell them about his wife, Remibias, and her strange experiences. He told them that Remibias had gone into a trance three different times and each time spoke in a strange voice and accent. This voice claimed to be Teresita Basa.

According to the husband, the spirit that took over Remibias described details about her murder, saying that a man named Allan Showery was the killer. Basa had worked with Showery, and he had come to her apartment to fix her television. While there, he decided to steal some of her jewelry, jewelry that Basa's spirit described. Showery stabbed and killed Basa during the robbery.

The police were incredulous. But they decided they had nothing to lose by investigating Showery. From Remibias's details, they were able to find the described jewelry and trace it back to Showery, who then confessed to her murder.

---

dence of the person they are visiting. According to Catholic priest Dan Reehil, "Demons lie and impersonate dead people."[14]

Maegan believes her family encountered a demon after moving into a new apartment. One night she was awakened by cries from her three-month-old daughter. When she got to the crib, the baby's legs were stuck in the crib's bars as if someone had been trying to pull her out.

A few nights later Maegan glanced at the nanny cam. What she saw terrified her. Now her three-year-old, in another bedroom, was being pulled from her bed. Maegan watched as an invisible entity placed her daughter onto the floor. Maegan ran into the bedroom, where she found her daughter sound asleep on the floor.

Maegan was frightened. She invited a friend over who believed she could communicate with spirits. She did not tell her friend about the strange occurrences happening in her home. The woman became uncomfortable as soon as she entered the apartment. She was especially troubled when she looked into the baby's room. She pointed at the rocking chair in the room and

While some ghosts are helpful, demons are believed to have malevolent intent.

said, "It's behind the rocking chair." The woman said she saw a tall, dark entity with red eyes and sharp teeth standing there. As they looked, Maegan's four-year-old niece came into the room, pointed at the rocking chair, and screamed, "What is that?"[15]

The last straw was when Maegan's three-year-old began talking about a soldier in her room who was nice during the day but mean at night. The family soon packed up and moved and never experienced strange events again. Maegan is sure the entity they encountered was some kind of demon.

Trickster Ghosts

According to psychic medium Jodi Livon, some ghosts play tricks on humans for no apparent reason. For instance, they turn lights on and off, move objects around, and open and close doors. The medium Kate had a disturbing experience with this kind of ghost. She was home alone watching TV one night when she heard her computer in the next room turn on. The computer was on a desk with a chair pushed up to it.

When Kate heard the computer, she looked toward the room and saw the computer's blueish light. She looked away, wondering what was going on, and then looked back. Now she could not see the light. She was horrified when she figured out why. The desk chair had somehow moved into the living room and was now facing Kate, blocking the light. How that had happened remained a mystery. Such mysteries are common when encountering ghosts. Spirits—whether malevolent, kind, or indifferent—often baffle people who are unsure of what these entities want or why they seem to appear to some individuals but not others. Investigating those mysteries is part of the enduring fascination with ghosts and the possibility of a life beyond death.

CHAPTER TWO

Making Themselves Known

People who see ghosts do not always report seeing hazy, transparent beings made popular in novels and films. Ghosts make themselves known in different ways, and not all of them are visual. Sometimes, they might be wisps of light that draw the eye or a felt presence that chills the spine. Household ghosts might remain unseen but knock on walls, open cabinets in another room, or fling objects to get attention. But regardless of how they manifest, they seem to want to interact with the living.

Dream Visions

Writer and astrologer Nina Kahn believes that sleep is an opportune time for spirits to visit. She says that dreams may create a small opening in a person's consciousness that allows entities from another realm to slip through.

Psychologist Anne Reith agrees. She says that "it is actually easier for spiritual entities of all kinds [such as] deceased loved ones, guides, [and] angels to communicate with us while we are sleeping, partly because you're more likely to be receptive to it in a dream than you would be in a waking state."[16]

Radio host Dave Schrader once spoke with a sleep technician who may have witnessed this firsthand. His job was to monitor sleeping patients to detect sleep illnesses. The technician said he regularly heard patients talking in their sleep as they dreamed. The peculiar thing, though, was that occasionally he would hear a different-sounding voice respond when no one else was in the room.

A woman from Wales named Sarah believes she had a spirit visit her dreams when she was seventeen. She had just moved with her mother into a new home that had been built on farmland near a small town.

Once there, Sarah began having a recurring dream about a tall man standing in the corner of her room. He was slim and wore a trench coat and a trilby hat, a kind that was popular in the 1900s. His body seemed to be blue. Most disturbing of all, though, was that whenever Sarah woke up from her dream, she would see the blue man standing in the corner of her room.

At first Sarah thought her dreams and visions were the result of the anxiety caused by so many changes in her life. She did not tell anyone about them because she did not want to worry her mother. Then her friend Becky came for a sleepover. In the morning Becky told Sarah that she had had a strange dream about a man in the room. Sarah jokingly said, "Oh, the man in the corner?" Becky looked at her in astonishment, saying, "Yes, Sarah, that's actually what I saw. A man in the corner in a trilby. And he was all blue."[17]

Sarah was stunned and made Becky promise to keep her dream a secret. Then one day a friend of Sarah's mother named Edwina came to visit while Sarah was gone. Edwina claimed to talk to spirits.

Edwina took a tour of the family's new home. When she got to Sarah's room, she refused to go in. Sarah's mother later told Sarah about it. Sarah laughingly asked if it was because her room was such a mess. Her mom said no, it was something

> "It is actually easier for spiritual entities of all kinds [such as] deceased loved ones, guides, [and] angels to communicate with us while we are sleeping, partly because you're more likely to be receptive to it in a dream than you would be in a waking state."[16]
>
> —Anne Reith, psychologist and director of the Institute for Mediumship, Psychic, Astrological, and Reiki Training

It is believed that spirits may be able to more easily visit people when they are asleep because dreams create a small opening in the consciousness that allows the spirit to slip through.

else. Sarah then said jokingly, "Oh, because of the man in the corner." Her mom looked shocked. She said, "Please don't tell me that he's blue and cold." Sarah nodded, adding that he wore a trilby and a long coat. "Yea," her mother replied, "that's exactly what Edwina said."[18]

This disturbed Sarah and her mother so much that they asked a priest over to bless the house. The priest told Sarah that when she saw the man, she should tell him it was time for him to move on. Sarah did this, and eventually he no longer appeared.

Ghostly Lights

Some ghosts are thought to appear as floating balls of light called orbs. According to medium Suzanne Geismann, orbs are essentially souls without bodies. Psychic medium Karen Frazier thinks that an orb's color can be meaningful. She says that a pink orb, for example, is sending a message of unconditional love and a yellow orb is communicating some sort of warning. A green orb can indicate a healing spirit.

Gettysburg, Pennsylvania, is the site of the deadliest battle ever fought during the American Civil War. Over fifty thousand men died there. The battlefield is considered one of the most haunted places in the United States. Today orbs are often seen in the area, and they also show up in photographs even when they are not seen at the time.

Photographer Lindsey Brisbine knows that orbs in photos can be produced by dust particles, insects, or water vapor. She also knows that some orbs in photos have no logical cause. She was especially intrigued by the ones she saw in her photos from a particular wedding. She talked about them on

An Imaginary Friend?

It is common for young children to have imaginary friends. But psychic medium Mary Ann Winkowski believes that this statement hides another truth. She says that "kids can see spirits that have crossed over and spirits that have not. . . . [Therefore] most of kids' imaginary playmates are not imaginary."

When Paulette's four-year-old daughter, Jessie, began talking about her invisible friend, Paulette thought it was a passing phase. Jessie called her friend Lisa, and they played together often. At the same time, weird things started happening in their house—wallpaper got ripped from walls, unaccountable footsteps were heard, and once Jessie was struck by a lamp in the night. One day Paulette found an inexplicable swarm of horseflies in her bathroom, a swarm that felt evil rather than natural. That was when Paulette realized that Lisa was some kind of entity. It might appear to Jessie as a child, but it was really something else. Paulette decided to move.

Just before leaving, she asked her neighbor whether anyone had ever reported hauntings in their house. Without hesitation, he replied, "Oh, you're talking about the little girl." He explained that his son had seen a little girl in the house when no one was living there.

Quoted in Fox 8 News, Cleveland, *The Ghost Whisperer*, YouTube, 2014. www.youtube.com/watch?v=kwlqsMUvGJw.

Quoted in *Spooked!* "Hidden in Plain Sight," May 24, 2024. https://play.prx.org/listen?ge=prx_409_a8552a5e-d36f-42ba-8239-de3a8b1bb6ea&uf=https%3A%2F%2Ffeeds.spookedpodcast.org.

Some ghosts appear to people as floating balls of light called orbs. These are believed to be souls without bodies.

The Chilling Podcast in an episode called "Orbs and Shadows with the Light Witch."

In several of the photos from this wedding, Brisbine saw a bright green light hovering near the groom. The light appeared in different photos of the groom in various places, but it did not appear in photos of other people in the same places. Brisbine knew that she had not seen it when she took the photographs. She also knew that the groom had a brother who had passed away. She wondered whether the orb might be the brother's spirit.

Brisbine showed the photos to the family without saying anything about the orbs. When the groom saw the pictures with orbs, he immediately pointed at them and said that was his brother. Then he told Brisbane that his brother had had green eyes.

Shadow People

Orbs are only one possible manifestation of spirits. Some ghosts appear as flat, dark figures that look human but lack any specific features. Author Heidi Hollis is one of the first people to use the name "shadow people" in reference to these ghosts. Shadow people are often described as being blacker than black. Some have glowing red eyes. Some wear hats. Most do not interact with people.

One theory says that shadow people are human spirits that are trapped in the living world and cannot move on. Another theory is that they are demons. Indeed, many people describe a feeling of malevolence emanating from them.

A man named Carson believes that he and his sisters saw a shadow man when they were young. They lived in a house at the edge of a forest. The bedrooms all had windows and balconies facing the woods.

One night when Carson was six years old, he woke up to hear his sisters yelling that there was someone outside their window. Carson looked out and saw a dark figure standing in the woods behind their house. Carson could not make out any features or clothing. All he could see was a dark silhouette peeking around a tree. It never moved, it simply stood and stared. It terrified Carson. The figure appeared several times over the next few months.

One night Carson's neighbors saw the man. They had called his mother wondering whether Carson's older brother was locked out of the house and trying to get in. They reported that a dark figure was standing on one of the home's balconies. But the brother was away at college. Carson's mother called the police, who came and looked around. They found nothing.

Carson's friend, who knew nothing about their mysterious visitor, saw him, too. One day as they played, the friend suddenly stopped and ran to Carson's sister, saying, "I saw a man standing on your porch."[19] The sister called the police, who came and checked, but again found nothing.

That was the last time the shadow man appeared. Carson's family was never able to explain what the figure was or why it had been there.

Humanlike Apparitions

Paranormal investigator Amy Bruni says that spirits are all around us and that people see them every day. They just do not know they are ghosts. According to Bruni, "We look [at] ghosts face to face and we have no idea that they are a dead person."[20] Paranormal blogger Sarah Chumacero agrees that many full-body apparitions look solid and realistic.

Jay, a woman who worked for the forest service, thinks she encountered a full-body apparition while working in the Arizona wilderness. Her job involved camping in remote areas and hiking into the backcountry to research bears.

One afternoon Jay climbed out of a canyon after a rain to arrive back on the road cold and wet. As she walked toward her truck, a man appeared out of nowhere with no other vehicle in sight. Jay was confused; she found it odd that after the downpour the man was wearing dry clothes, perfectly white tennis shoes, and a clean shirt.

> "We look [at] ghosts face to face and we have no idea that they are a dead person."[20]
>
> —Amy Bruni, author, television producer, and actress

She was immediately uneasy. The man told Jay he had hiked there. Again, this seemed impossible. He then told Jay he was lost and needed a ride.

Jay tried calling for help on her radio but had no reception. This was not unusual. She decided she would leave the man with supplies and radio his location to her headquarters once she had a connection. Jay got into her truck and rolled down her window to tell the man about her plan.

The next thing she remembers is driving down the road with the man sitting in her passenger seat. She had no idea when he had gotten into the truck. Confused, Jay stopped the truck and told the man to get out. He did. She watched him walk off into the woods, laughing the whole way. Jay then drove 5 miles (8 km) farther to her solitary camp in a meadow.

Once there, she sat in her truck facing the edge of the meadow. She tried her radio again, and this time it worked. As she

The Ghost of Abraham Lincoln

The full-body apparition of Abraham Lincoln seems to be a regular visitor to the White House. First Lady Grace Coolidge was the first person to report seeing him. She said she once saw him staring out a window in the Oval Office. He was dressed in black with his hands clasped behind his back. He turned and looked at her and then disappeared.

President Theodore Roosevelt experienced Lincoln, too, saying, "I see him in different rooms and in the halls." When Queen Wilhelmina of the Netherlands stayed at the White House, she answered a knock on her door to find Lincoln standing there wearing his famous top hat. She promptly fainted.

One night while visiting the White House, British prime minister Winston Churchill walked into his bedroom and saw Lincoln standing at the fireplace. Eleanor Roosevelt's secretary reported seeing Lincoln sitting on a bed pulling on his boots. Mrs. Roosevelt herself described feeling his presence when she worked in her study. Her study just happened to be Lincoln's old bedroom.

The last known Lincoln sighting was in the early 1980s, when a White House worker saw Lincoln sitting in a chair, hands folded and legs crossed. The worker blinked, and Lincoln was gone.

Quoted in American Hauntings, "The Haunted White House: Ghosts of America's Executive Mansion." www.americanhauntingsink.com.

---

reported into headquarters, she looked out at the meadow. There was the man, walking toward her.

Jay was terrified. There was no way he could have walked there so quickly from where she had dropped him off. Suddenly, her truck shut down. She glanced at the dashboard in surprise and then looked back out the window. Now the man was much closer, having crossed the meadow at an unbelievable speed. Jay blinked and the man was at her window.

Then the man was shouting at her. Over and over he yelled, "Give me my hat back now!"[21] Jay noticed that his baseball cap was still on the truck's dash, and she shoved it through the window. He took it and walked away, again moving unreasonably fast.

Suddenly Jay's truck started up. She jumped out, grabbed her gear, and threw it into the truck. She drove back to headquarters and promptly quit her job.

Monstrous Entities

While Jay's experience seemed threatening, thankfully the man did not hurt her. Michelle Belanger says that malevolent spirits—such as demons—have more wicked intentions. She believes that demons can take on different forms. She says that in the spirit world, "form is also a language and method of communication and therefore changeable."[22] Some people report seeing hideous monsters that horrify them. Others report swirling mists or fogs that feel evil. At times these mists morph into some kind of frightening being.

Many people have had encounters with malevolent spirits that had wicked intentions and morphed into frightening beings.

On an episode of the *Otherworld* podcast titled "The Night Hag," a man named Alec shared his terrifying experience with morphing figures. When young, Alec would get up in the night and feel compelled to wander around his house. While on these midnight forays, he would frequently encounter a figure standing in the downstairs hallway. The figure had a white face that was cracked and old. It had black hair and long, flowing black arms that did not seem to have an end.

Alec would stand watching this being, frozen with fear. As he did, shadows would ripple and rise from the floor into 3-D beings. Spears would shoot from their bodies and stab Alec in his chest as if they were trying to get inside him. He wanted to run and scream but he was unable to move.

In a final encounter, the being came to Alec in his bed. This time, instead of arms and legs, it had tentacles that stabbed at him. For the first time ever, he was able to yell at the figure, telling it to get out. Then there was a tremor and a loud explosion inside Alec's head. The figure disappeared, and that was the last time he experienced the entity.

Alex's experience demonstrates that encounters with ghostly beings can prove fearful. Yet others are so unobtrusive that their appearances can be overlooked or attributed to the imagination. These brushes with spectral forces spark people's interests in the unknowable, and the variety of manifestations add to the uncanny feeling that that the ghostly realm is one that the living are not meant to rationalize; it will forever remain—in inexplicably opening doors or previously unseen orbs of light caught on film—just outside understanding.

How Do They Do It?

People who believe in ghosts often wonder just how they materialize into the earthly world. There are several theories as to the methods used by entities to make themselves appear. Many people think that ghosts are able to appear by connecting with people who have psychic—or psi—abilities. Jeff Tarrant is a neuroscientist who believes that people who see ghosts are using a special part of their brains in ways that scientists do not yet understand. He says, "I have seen enough to make me believe that our minds are capable of much more than most of us dare to imagine. While we may not fully understand how or why, it seems clear to me now that psi abilities are a natural and normal part of human experience, and that scientists should dedicate more time and resources to exploring them."[23] Thus, it may not be a product of ghostly will but a living person's willingness and openness to psychic connections that facilitate such appearances.

> "While we may not fully understand how or why, it seems clear to me now that psi abilities are a natural and normal part of human experience, and that scientists should dedicate more time and resources to exploring them."[23]
>
> —Jeff Tarrant, neuroscientist

Psychic Talents

Kerrie Erwin says that people with these psychic talents emanate an energy that is like a beacon to spirits. Ghosts flock to the

Country-western singer Loretta Lynn, pictured here at an awards show, believed she had psychic talents and had passed them on to her children.

beacon and connect with these individuals. Many people think that these sorts of psychic abilities run in families.

The family of the late country-western singer Loretta Lynn may be one of those families. Lynn's mother believed she had psychic talents, and Lynn herself had seen ghosts since childhood. As an adult, Lynn bought a home in Tennessee that had been used as a hospital during the Civil War. She regularly saw and heard ghosts in the house and on the property. Doors opened and closed by themselves, she heard unexplainable footsteps, and she once saw an unknown woman crying on her bedroom balcony. Lynn was convinced she was experiencing the spirits of those who had suffered there during the war.

Lynn believed she passed her psychic abilities on to her children. When her daughters were growing up, they regularly reported seeing Confederate soldiers inside the house. And they often saw a strange woman standing by their bed. Lynn thought this was the same woman she had seen crying on the balcony. Lynn's son saw apparitions, too. He once complained of his boots being tugged off his feet by a soldier as he napped.

Energy Borrowers

Another theory that explains ghostly appearances proposes that ghosts find and use energy from the living world to appear. Ghost hunters regularly report that although their electrical equipment is completely charged and functioning before an investigation, it loses power or breaks down soon after an investigation begins. They attribute this to spirits borrowing energy to materialize.

Mary Ann Winkowski says she has seen ghosts appear on computer screens while conducting video readings. These ghosts will nod or shake their heads in answer to her questions. One spirit even showed Winkowski the last four numbers of her own Social Security number to verify her identity.

A woman named Wendy believes that her father, Harry, used the telephone to communicate with her after his death. She had moved into his house after he died, and soon after, she turned his telephone service off. Even so, calls kept coming into his phone. Whenever Wendy answered, she would hear nothing but static.

Frustrated, Wendy called the phone company and was told that the line was not in service. Calls to it and from it were impossible. Indeed, when she called her father's number from her own phone, a message told her that the line had been disconnected. But she still got calls.

One day when the phone rang, it finally made sense to Wendy. She believed it was her father calling to communicate with her. "Oh, my God! It's Dad!"[24] she shouted into the phone. Although there was still nothing but static on the line, she spoke into the noise, talking at him. The static would get louder and softer as if he were speaking back. She says she felt like he was telling her that he had been doing this for months.

Erwin says that spirits can also use the heat energy in an environment to manifest. Cold spots are commonly reported by people who feel haunted. They often report that an area of their home remains cold no matter what is done to heat it.

Winkowski says that people themselves are another source of energy for spirits. She says that if "you have a ghost in the house, you are going to be tired all the time. So it's almost like they're an energy vampire sucking the energy out of you."[25]

Electronic Voice Phenomena

Believing that ghosts can use radio waves to speak with people, ghost hunters often use sound recording devices to capture spirit voices. The radio waves are not heard by the human ear, but their presence is detected by the equipment. When played back, they often sound like static. But ghost hunters believe they sometimes hear words spoken by spirits in the static. This is called an electronic voice phenomenon (EVP).

To obtain an EVP, researchers turn on their recording device and begin asking questions. They pause between questions to give spirits time to answer. Later they play back their recordings to see whether a spirit has responded.

One night, paranormal investigator Adam Berry and his friends were trying to capture EVPs in a cemetery. Berry walked toward a crypt and began recording. He asked, "Hello, anyone there?" and waited a few minutes. Then he played back the recording. After hearing his question asked, there came a voice saying, "Help me."

Berry and his friends were astonished. According to one, "When we actually heard an answer on the recorder, it was confirmation for me. There was undeniable evidence: I was there, I knew that none of us who were alive had said anything."

Adam Berry, *Goodbye Hello*. New York: Regalo Press, 2023, p. 37.

Winkowski says that spirits can also take energy from people who are feeling extreme anxiety or fear. She notes that ghosts are also found around large groups of people because there is so much energy present.

Residual Hauntings

Besides feeding on living energy, ghosts might also result from energy imprinted on the environment. This is often referred to as a residual haunting, and it happens when energy from a natural event is released into a location and is somehow recorded by that environment. The theory suggests that a person's actions are recorded—like a tape recorder records voices—onto rocks, stones, walls, or other objects in the environment. These impressions are more likely to be recorded if an event is especially traumatic. The energy is then replayed in the environment long after the living participants are gone. According to author Justin Bienvenue, residual hauntings are the most common kind of ghostly experience. He says this kind of haunting explains footsteps and other ghostly noises that people frequently hear.

Ghosts in residual hauntings do not interact with the living. They will perform an action over and over, apparently unaware of the humans around them. They seem to walk through walls and float through the air because the material world has changed since the recording was made. A residual ghost is stuck in a loop of behavior that is not happening in real time—it is simply a recording being played back repeatedly.

The Stanley Hotel in Estes Park, Colorado, may have residual hauntings. This is the hotel that inspired Stephen King's novel *The Shining*. Built in 1909, the hotel seems to regularly host invisible visitors. Guests often report hearing piano music coming from the hotel's concert hall when no one is there. And guests who stay on the fourth floor often say they hear children laughing and run-

The Stanley Hotel in Estes Park, Colorado, is believed to have residual hauntings. This hotel inspired author Stephen King's novel The Shining.

ning in the hallway when no one is present. The fourth floor just happens to be where guests from the early 1900s housed their nannies and children.

Portals

While some ghosts may be environmental playback, others might appear on earth through portals between dimensions. Some paranormal researchers propose that the space between dimensions has special qualities, and some of this space may be more porous than others. Thus, there may be locations where the space is so thin that "doorways" allow ghosts to travel into the living world. The late paranormal researcher Rosemary Ellen Guiley believed that these portals "are all over the planet [and are places] where the boundaries between dimensions are very permeable."[26]

> "[Ghost portals] are all over the planet [and are places] where the boundaries between dimensions are very permeable."[26]
>
> —Rosemary Ellen Guiley, spiritualist writer

Annie Wilder believes her Minnesota home is some kind of portal. Soon after buying it, she heard voices and poundings on the walls and was once pinned down by an unseen force. Psychic Linda Drake visited the house and told Wilder, "This house is filled with 'doorways.' It's like Grand Central Station for ghosts."[27]

Television producer Brian Dellis went to the house to film a Halloween show. While there he saw strange happenings, including lights turning on and off for no reason. When he drove home from the filming, he smelled a strange, minty pipe smoke in his van even though he was alone. He worried that a ghost had attached itself to him. Formerly a skeptic, the visit convinced Dellis that Wilder's house was haunted.

Wilder later had more psychics come through her house. They took photographs and then sat in a circle to communicate with the spirits. They felt two names coming though—Emma and LeDuc. They did not know who Emma was, but LeDuc was a well-known town resident. When Dellis looked through photos the psychics had taken, he found one with an image in a mirror.

Ghostly Attachments

In 1972 an Eastern Airlines flight crashed, killing over one hundred people, including pilots Robert Loft and Donald Repo. Airplane parts were later retrieved from the crash, and any that were still usable were put into other aircraft.

Soon after, strange things began to happen in the airplanes that had received these parts. In one plane, for example, a passenger dressed like a pilot suddenly appeared in an empty seat. The man was not on the passenger list. He sat silently, ignoring questions from flight attendants. Finally, the pilot came to talk to the man, who still did not respond. The pilot, though, immediately recognized the man—it was Loft.

Repo was also seen on flights. One day a flight attendant was preparing food and saw Repo's reflection in an oven door. She called two other crew members, who saw the reflection, too. They then heard the reflection say, "Watch out for fire on this plane." Although that flight did not have any problems, one of the plane's engines did catch fire on its return flight.

There were other ghostly happenings on other airplanes that had received salvaged parts, too. Eastern Airlines removed all the recovered parts from various airplanes, and eventually the sightings stopped.

Quoted in Paranormal Catalog, "The Ghosts of Flight 401," October 14, 2023. www.paranormalcatalog.net.

Dellis went to the local historical society to compare the image with photos of LeDuc. He believed it was the same man.

Conjuring Ghosts

Some people believe that ghosts come into the world of the living—whether through portals or other means—because they are invited. There are a variety of ways people call forth ghosts. One is through séances. During a séance a medium sits with a group of people, and they ask spirits to appear and answer questions about their past lives and their current experiences. Séances are often performed to let the living know that their loved ones who have passed on are at peace.

Ghost hunting is another way to invite spirits into this world. During a ghost hunt, investigators visit places that are thought to be haunted and try to communicate with the ghosts. The investigators often use special equipment, such as night vision goggles and meters that measure electrical pulses or temperature changes, hoping to identify a ghost's presence.

Another popular way of conjuring ghosts into the living world is through the Ouija board, a flat board that has the alphabet written across it. Users then place a device called a planchette on the board. A planchette is a small pointed board with four short legs and a window cut into it. Two people place their fingertips on the planchette and ask the spirits a question. If a spirit is present, it guides the planchette to letters to spell out an answer.

Some people believe that Ouija boards attract evil spirits. According to Catholic priest Dan Reehil, "When asking a board for information about a deceased person, or a life decision, [demons] are all too happy to embed themselves into your life."[28]

Michelle Belanger, however, believes that various methods of calling spirits into the living world can be done safely by those

A Ouija board is a flat board with the alphabet written on it. It is a popular way of communicating with spirits.

who know how to protect themselves. She says, "All of these are just tools. I could use a hammer to bash somebody's skull in or to hammer a nail and build a house . . . they are all merely tools."[29]

Indeed, Elle Grace had a pleasant experience with a spirit apparently called forth by a Ouija board. When her mother and aunt were children, they moved into a home that had been built in the 1890s. One day they were playing with a Ouija board when a spirit that called itself Mrs. Moon came through. Mrs. Moon said she had once lived in the house. Her husband had died of a heart attack, and her son had died in World War I. She had then taken on boarders to support herself. Elle Grace's mother and aunt were overcome with curiosity, so they visited their library and found public records that verified everything Mrs. Moon had told them.

Elle Grace's parents ended up buying the house, and she grew up there. She always felt a presence in her home, and objects were always moving around in odd ways. Her mother attributed the strange happenings to Mrs. Moon. Elle Grace was never scared of Mrs. Moon and thought of her as a benevolent presence.

The Mystery Remains

Theories abound as to the mechanics of just how unearthly spirits manifest in the living world. Perhaps there is no one method they use, or perhaps different kinds of ghosts use different means. People encounter shades and specters in so many locations that it is difficult to determine whether a ghostly rider on a battlefield materializes in the same way as a comforting spiritual presence stands and then fades by a relative's bedside. If ghosts are real, the physics of how they make themselves appear is still one of many unanswered questions about them.

CHAPTER FOUR

Ghosts of Many Cultures

Throughout history, almost every culture in the world has told stories about ghosts. Many are entities that are unique to them. But stories about some of the same ghosts appear in many different cultures. Each culture may call the ghost a different name, but their characteristics and behaviors are similar.

The White Lady

The white lady is a ghost that is told about in many different cultures. Sometimes she is the spirit of a woman who has had a tragic death. Sometimes she is a heartbroken lover searching the world for her former sweetheart. The white lady may haunt a place, bring misfortune to those she encounters, or perform an act of kindness. But she is always dressed in white.

One such story has been passed down for generations among the Native Americans of New Mexico. It is about a beautiful Mexican woman named Manuela, whose betrothed, Hernando de Luna, left her to join Francisco Coronado's 1542 exploration of the American Southwest. De Luna was wounded in a battle with Apache Indians somewhere around what is now White Sands National Monument. Hearing this, Manuela set off for the dunes to find him and nurse him back to health.

According to the tale, Manuela was never again seen alive. Her spirit, though, still wanders the sands, looking for de Luna. She is now called Pavla Blanca, or La Pavura Blanca, meaning

> "It is believed that the ghost of Manuela still haunts the dunes of the great White Sands, just after sunset, in her flowing white wedding gown, to seek her love, lost and buried beneath the eternal dunes."[30]
>
> —National Park Service pamphlet
> *A Lingering Love*

"the white dread." The National Park Service recounts the tale, saying, "It is believed that the ghost of Manuela still haunts the dunes of the great White Sands, just after sunset, in her flowing white wedding gown, to seek her love, lost and buried beneath the eternal dunes."[30]

In *American Ghost Stories*, author Michael A. Kozlowski tells about a man named Robert who thinks he saw Pavla Blanca while hiking through White Sands National Monument. He was about halfway through his hike when he realized he had lost his way. The wind was blowing, causing the dunes to shift and Robert to lose sight of trail markers. Soon each dune looked like the other, and Robert had no idea where he was. Night was coming on, and Robert was not prepared to be out overnight. He began to panic.

Then he noticed a woman on the next sand dune. She was wearing a white dress that was blowing about her body. It was strange clothing for a hiker, but Robert had few choices. He hiked

Many cultures have variations on a story of a ghost called the white lady. Sometimes she is the spirit of a woman who has had a tragic death, and in other stories she is a heartbroken lover.

toward her to ask for help. However, when he reached the top of the dune she had been standing on, she was gone. Confused, Robert looked around. Then he saw her. She was standing on the next dune. Again, he moved toward her. Again, she disappeared only to appear on a nearby dune.

Robert continued following the woman. Each time he drew close, she would disappear and reappear on another dune. Finally, Robert looked up and the woman was nowhere to be seen. What he did see was a sign pointing to the trailhead. He hiked toward it, never seeing the lady in white again. Robert feels sure the apparition had guided him to safety.

The Banshee

Old Irish legends tell of a creature called the banshee, the ghost of a young woman who was murdered. Her spirit now roams the earth, warning people when someone in their family is about to die. The warning comes in the form of a terrifying wail that is so high pitched that people can barely stand hearing it.

Sometimes the banshee is said to be a beautiful young woman with long white or red hair. At other times she is an old woman with dirty gray hair, long fingernails, and sharp, rotted teeth.

People still believe in the banshee. Writing for a website about Irish folklore, Serena retells a story about a woman who remembered an incident from her childhood. The story goes that the woman's uncle was walking home from a gathering late one night. Near home he came across an old woman on the road. She was dressed in black with a veil over her face, and she was wailing. When he went to comfort her, she moved away but pointed at his house and continued crying. The man told his mother about the encounter, but she said little. Three days later, the mother's brother died in his sleep. Afterward, the mother told the man the woman he had met was the banshee.

A man named Brent also thinks he encountered the banshee and talked about it on an episode of the *Monsters Among Us* podcast. Brent is of Irish descent and at the time was living with

Night Visitors

The night hag is a ghoul often described as a wrinkled old woman with long hair and an ancient appearance. She crawls into people's beds as they sleep and climbs onto their chests. The victims wake up but cannot move or breathe because of her weight.

Almost every culture has a version of the night hag. In Fiji the night hag is called *kana tevoro*, which means "to be eaten by a demon." It is sometimes thought of as a recently deceased relative who comes back because of some kind of unfinished business.

According to Albanian folktales, Mokthi is a harmless male spirit with a golden hat. He visits sleeping women and prevents them from moving. He will grant them a wish if they can take his hat.

The Japanese call the night visitor *kanashibari*, a word that means "bound or fastened in metal." Some Arab cultures warn that the night hag is a demon that not only sits on people but also chokes them. In Old English, the demon who sat on the chest of the sleeping was known as a "mare." This word eventually morphed into the word *nightmare*.

---

his mother in an apartment. One night a high-pitched scream woke him up. His mother was already awake, and he asked her whether she had heard a scream. She said no, but that she had just received a call from the hospital. Brent's uncle was there because he had had a seizure and fallen. The uncle soon died. Brent believes the scream he heard was the banshee coming to warn his family of his uncle's impending death.

The Flying Head

The Iroquois and Wyandot Indians of the American Northeast both tell stories about a ghost called the flying head. This ghoul is cursed with a hunger that never goes away. It appears as a head with a large mouth, sharp teeth, and long dark hair. The flying head is said to have wings coming out of its cheeks.

One Reddit user wonders whether he encountered the flying head when he and two friends went for a hike. About half an hour into their hike, they ventured into the surrounding forest. As the sun began to set, they turned back. Then suddenly, they heard

> "About 30 feet in the air we saw, what I can only describe as a human head. It had long, oily black hair, and hollow, pale eyes. The skin, like something out of a horror movie, was drooping off the skull, hanging down the sides. . . . Out of the side of the head, around the cheeks or ears . . . were smallish bat-like wings."[31]
>
> —Frameglasseye, Reddit user

a flapping of wings like a large bird or bat. They turned to look, and the hiker described what appeared: "About 30 feet in the air we saw, what I can only describe as a human head. It had long, oily black hair, and hollow, pale eyes. The skin, like something out of a horror movie, was drooping off the skull, hanging down the sides. . . . Out of the side of the head, around the cheeks or ears . . . were smallish bat-like wings."[31] The entity did not seem to notice the hikers. It simply flew off into the forest as they watched in shock. The friends were so traumatized by their experience that they never talked about it again.

Similar stories of flying heads are told in Asia. The Krasue of Thailand is thought to be the spirit of a cursed, sinful woman. The *penanggalan* of Malay culture is almost identical, though it is thought to be the ghost of a woman who practiced black magic. Both now appear as the heads of women with entrails dangling below the throat, and these monstrosities savor raw flesh.

The penanggalan, as pictured here, is from Malay culture. It is believed to be the ghost of a woman who practiced black magic.

The Pontianak

The Pontianak is another female ghost from Southeast Asia that has been around for generations. There are many variations of her story. In most versions, the Pontianak is a woman who died during childbirth. This left her seeking revenge for her untimely death, usually by killing and eating innocent men.

According to the legends, the scent of flowers often precedes the appearance of the Pontianak. Then the ghost manifests as a beautiful woman with long black hair in a white dress. Her beauty draws a man to her, and then she transforms into a hideous being and eviscerates her victim with long, sharp fingernails.

Uniquely, the spirit of the Pontianak is said to inhabit rubber trees during the day. An area in northern Singapore was once the home of a famous rubber plantation. The plantation was eventually overtaken by the growth of the city, and its trees were cut down to make room for roads, homes, and buildings. Many people believe the Pontianak had lived on the plantation and became angered that her home was destroyed. The area, in fact, is known as one of Singapore's most haunted locations. People who live nearby often report hearing voices calling to them. Some have even seen a ghostly woman walking around.

While working as a Singapore policeman, Reddit user Dumas thinks he encountered the Pontianak. One night while on patrol, he and his partners came across a fallen tree, so they got out to move it. Dumas lifted one end while the others lifted the other. Suddenly, his partners screamed and dropped the trunk. Then Dumas heard the leaves of a nearby tree rustle loudly. By the time Dumas set down his side of the tree, the others were in the jeep screaming at him to get in. Once he was inside, they all sped off.

Dumas's partners were clearly disturbed. One asked him whether he had seen anything. When he said no, they told him that as they were lifting the trunk, they saw the Pontianak come out of the fallen tree and jump into another tree near them.

The Day of the Dead

Many Mexican families celebrate a multiday holiday at the end of October called the Day of the Dead. They believe that there are three days when the border between the spirit world and the physical world dissolves. This is when spirits wake up and visit their loved ones.

On the Day of the Dead, families honor their loved ones with altars in their homes or gifts at their grave sites. Candles, marigolds, tortillas, and fruit are common offerings. Toys are bought for children who have died. All the gifts are intended to entice the deceased to visit. Some people like to scatter flower petals from a grave to their homes so the dead can find their way there.

In some places it is a tradition to spend a day at the cemetery to picnic and play music. Some families even spend the night at a grave to be close to the departed.

Calveras, or skulls, are common decorations for this celebration. Many are made of wood or paper and brightly decorated. Some *calveras* are made of sugar and eaten as candy. The Day of the Dead is a pleasant holiday when loved ones share memories and honor the deceased.

Poltergeists

A poltergeist is a spirit from German folklore known for making noise. The word *poltergeist*, in fact, means "noisy spirit" or "rumbling ghost." It is sometimes thought of as mischievous, knocking things over or moving objects around. But the mild, playful acts can escalate into frightening behaviors. Sometimes poltergeists throw objects or even bite and pinch people.

Although the name comes from German tales, poltergeists seem to haunt people in countries all over the world. Some paranormal researchers believe these ghosts steal energy from the real world. According to podcaster Forrest Burgess, many poltergeist cases are said to center on a troubled adolescent and use that child's emotional energy to cause mischief.

This may have happened to a young Polish girl named Joasia Gajewski. Gajewski was extremely close to her maternal grandmother, who passed away in 1982 when Gajewski was twelve. Not long after, strange events began happening. Things in Gajewski's home moved by themselves from one room to another.

Objects were thrown around. Glass appeared out of nowhere and exploded in the air, often cutting Gajewski.

Several people witnessed these events, and most were left baffled as to the cause. One police officer who investigated wrote in his report, "There is inexplicable physical phenomena happening. And spontaneous movement of objects."[32] Electrical engineers, chemists, physicians, and other scientists all visited Gajewski, trying to figure out what was happening. None were ever able to explain the strange occurrences. However, some researchers on the case believed that the destruction attributed to the poltergeist was really produced by Gajewski's unconscious mind's telekinetic powers, spurred on by her anger and grief. They maintain that once Gajewski grew up and married, the events ceased because her inner turmoil subsided.

Poltergeists are noisy spirits known for making mischief. Many cases are said to be caused by the emotional energy of troubled adolescents.

Not all poltergeists are so violent. One Reddit user recalls a more good-natured poltergeist that was a regular visitor to her and her neighbor. She tells how she would come home and find things in strange places. There would be toilet paper in the refrigerator or laundry detergent in the bathtub. Once the neighbor called to say she could not find a gallon of milk. After looking around, they finally found it on her back steps. This activity continued for the entire two years the woman lived there, and she was never able to explain what was happening. Both neighbors simply decided they had a poltergeist.

Connected to the Living World

Ghost stories have appeared in all cultures and across the centuries. Some ghosts have shared characteristics across cultures, leaving paranormal investigators to wonder whether the disparate cultures are dealing with similar spirits. These ghosts often are associated with common human emotions like anger and grief, and perhaps those feelings are strong enough to draw spirits or keep them tied to the living. Regardless, many of these stories have lingered into modern times, and some are still held in reverence by cultures that venerate the dead and pay heed to the warnings and wisdom of ancestors who have moved into another realm.

CHAPTER FIVE

Science Explains Ghosts

According to science, ghosts defy the laws of physics, so they cannot be real. For example, a weightless, ethereal being cannot make noisy footsteps. And science knows of no mechanism by which dead people can materialize into the world of the living.

The existence of ghosts also defies the laws of logic. If ghosts were real, more people would experience them. Real things are seen by everyone, not just part of the population. Instead of explaining strange occurrences as visits from another realm, scientists give several explanations for what is really happening to people who believe they have experienced a ghost.

Explanations from the Physical World

The first explanation science gives for ghostly phenomena is that encounters have a real-life physical cause. Breezes or drafts can make doors open and close. Faulty wiring can cause lights to flicker. And changes in temperatures and humidity can cause wood and other materials to expand and contract, often making popping or creaking sounds.

Ghostly images can also be explained scientifically. Many are the result of reflections or misidentified objects. For example, one Michigan family feared they had a ghost when they saw a filmy figure pass through their toddler's room on a nanny cam. But researcher Kenny Biddle showed them what had really happened. He found that a combination of reflections, including one from a television program that had been paused, and the night vision feature on the camera itself was creating an eerie distortion of one of the parents moving through the room.

Electromagnetic fields (EMFs) may be another natural cause of ghostly experiences. An EMF is an invisible area of energy made when an electrical field interacts with a magnetic field. Many things can create an EMF, including power lines, computers, cell phone towers, and cell phones themselves. Small changes in EMFs can be caused by nearby metal objects, magnets, storms, or even the earth's rotation. Although humans do not always feel these changes, some devices are very sensitive to them, and a small change can cause them to turn on or off or to exhibit a malfunction. This could be interpreted as a ghost.

In addition, some people are especially sensitive to EMFs. This sensitivity can cause various psychological symptoms, some of which are the same feelings people report having when they feel haunted. In one study, even the low level of EMFs given off by an alarm clock caused one person to see apparitions.

One explanation science gives for ghostly activities actually have real-life physical causes, such as energy from cell phone towers.

Frauds and Hoaxes

Skeptics understand that playing to people's fascination with the paranormal can be a profitable business. Haunted places attract visitors, increasing their revenue. People who say they can contact spirits often charge money for their services, and some people are willing to pay a lot to communicate with deceased loved ones. And the detection tools used by ghost hunters can cost hundreds of dollars. Overall, because there are people willing to pay money to see ghosts, there are also people willing to take advantage of them. Hoaxers are common in the paranormal field, and skeptics have been exposing them for years.

Two famous fraudsters were the Fox sisters. In the mid-1800s, these sisters claimed they could talk with the dead. As word of their talent spread, a third sister decided to cash in on their talents. She began setting up large demonstrations and charging a fee to watch. During the shows, the sisters would ask spirits questions and receive answers via knocks.

Many years after their fame had faded, one of the sisters confessed that the demonstrations were, in fact, staged. The sisters had become masters at cracking their knuckles and toes to make the knocks they said were responses from spirits. However, even after the confession, unscrupulous writers continued to credit the sisters with amazing powers, feeding the growing interest in parapsychology that their stories helped generate.

Modern-day hoaxers have other kinds of tricks to fool people into thinking they are communicating with ghosts. Reporter Matt Kielty explains one hoax used by some ghost hunters. For this trick, ghost hunters tell their clients that if a spirit is present, it will turn a flashlight on and off to communicate. They then set out a flashlight and begin asking the ghost questions. Eerily, the flashlight turns on and off periodically, seemingly in response to the questions.

However, there is an explanation for why this is happening that has nothing to do with ghosts. It involves a certain kind of flashlight that uses a plastic piece to activate the light. Before

The Fox sisters, as shown here in an 1852 photo, became famous for talking to the dead. It was later revealed that their demonstrations were staged.

beginning the hoax, fraudsters turn the flashlight on until the bulb inside gets hot. They then slightly unscrew the top until the flashlight turns off. Once the light is off, the connective plastic component cools down. As it cools, it contracts and makes the light turn back on.

Now the light heats up the inside again. This causes the plastic to expand. The expansion turns the flashlight off. This cycle will continue for some time. As it does, the ghost hunters ask the "spirits" questions and get "answers" via the light switching on and off.

Mustafa Gatollari has been conducting paranormal investigations for over twenty years. In so doing, he has found other ways investigators fake evidence. For example, radiating electromagnetic

Thomas Edison's Spirit Phone

Thomas Edison was one of America's most prolific inventors. He invented the phonograph, a motion picture camera, and one of the first lightbulbs.

Near the end of his life, Edison was working on a "spirit phone," a mechanism that would be used to speak with the dead. Of it, he said, "I have been at work for some time building an apparatus to see if it is possible for personalities which have left this Earth to communicate with us."

Edison's spirit phone was a projector-like machine that emitted a thin beam of light onto a photoelectric cell. The device was meant to detect any ghost moving through the beam.

In 1920 Edison invited mediums and scientists to his lab to test out his work. Hours passed and nothing happened. Edison was not discouraged. He continued working on his project until his death, but he never connected with the dead.

Interestingly, Edison and his friend William Walter Dinwiddie had once agreed that the first one to die would try to contact the other from the beyond. And though Dinwiddie passed away about a decade before Edison, there is no evidence that Edison received any kind of after-death communication from his friend.

Quoted in Michele Debczak, "When Thomas Edison Tried Besting Nikola Tesla by Building a Spirit Phone," *Mental Floss*, October 25, 2019. www.mentalfloss.com.

---

pods are electronic sensors often used in ghost-hunting television shows. They are supposed to light up when a ghost passes by. These pods, however, are extremely sensitive and are set off by any nearby electronics. Television equipment and even cell phones can activate a pod. This makes their use as ghost detectors useless in most situations.

Sleep Paralysis

Not all scientific explanations expose purposeful trickery. Sleep paralysis is a condition resulting from a glitch in a normal and healthy brain function, causing confusion between the brain and the body. Sleep paralysis causes a person to feel paralyzed and helpless.

Neuroscientist Baland Jalal explains that vivid dreams occur during a stage of sleep characterized by rapid eye movement (REM). During REM sleep, the brain uses chemicals to shut down the body so it cannot act on a dream. This keeps dreamers from hurting themselves.

At times there is a problem in the body's functioning, and a person wakes up during REM sleep while brain chemicals are keeping the body immobile. This makes a fully awake person feel paralyzed. This state is known as sleep paralysis.

Sleep paralysis can be a terrifying experience, since it leaves a person feeling unable to escape a perceived danger from a dream. This condition affects about one in every five people, so many people face this uncomfortable terror.

One woman named Jordyn Samper knows how scary sleep paralysis can be. She suffers from it about two times a month. Her experiences usually start with seeing a large, dark figure with horns and red eyes in the corner of her room. Sometimes the figure moves to her bed and sits on her chest, making her feel as if she cannot breathe. Samper says, "It's scary not being able to move with a demon watching you, but I remind myself it's not real and hyper focus on trying to move my pinky finger. Once I do that, it's pretty immediate to snap out of."[33] Samper has not actually been visited by a night hag but unfortunately suffers from a common medical condition.

> "It's scary not being able to move with a demon watching you, but I remind myself it's not real and hyper focus on trying to move my pinky finger. Once I do that, it's pretty immediate to snap out of."[33]
>
> —Jordyn Samper, experiencer of sleep paralysis

Apophenia

Electronic voice phenomena (EVPs), the eerie voices seemingly captured on recordings, might also have scientific explanations. Scientists say that EVPs are simply electrical static that comes from electronics in the environment. When listening to this static, the brain then seeks out patterns, patterns that are most often configured as words because the brain understands speech sounds. Scientists call this apophenia. Apophenia is the human tendency to look for patterns in things that are random.

When ghost hunters capture a believed EVP, they often share it with a second person, telling that person what they have heard. This person, then, is predisposed to hearing the same thing.

Biddle tells about just such a case. It involved an EVP that was supposedly generated by a portrait of a woman called Annie. While housed in a museum of paranormal artifacts, the museum's website called the portrait one of its most powerful entities. The museum reported that investigators once captured an EVP near the portrait that answered the question, "What is your name?" with a voice replying "Annie."[34]

When Biddle learned that the EVP had been captured using a radio that was modified to scan through several radio frequencies,

EVPs, the eerie voices seemingly captured through sound equipment, might have scientific explanations. Scientists say that EVPs are simply electrical static that the brain interprets as a speech pattern.

he became skeptical. This kind of scanning allows the recorder to capture short clips from many different radio broadcasts. Biddle believes this is what happened in the Annie case. Ghost hunters had already connected the name Annie to the portrait, so apophenia could cause believers to think they heard the name Annie in a string of random words from various radio programs.

The brain also looks for patterns in what it sees. This is a kind of apophenia called pareidolia. Pareidolia helps humans make sense of their world. As psychologist Stephen Hupp explains, pareidolia happens when we see faces or figures in the clouds. He goes on to say that pareidolia can also make "random shapes and shadows in a dark house look like a ghost."[35]

Ghostly Hallucinations

Hallucinations may be another reason people think they have experienced a ghost. A hallucination is an image created in the brain that people believe is occurring in real life. While they are tricks of the brain, hallucinations seem very real to the people experiencing them.

Hallucinations have many causes. Certain drugs can cause them. Mental illnesses can cause them. Hallucinations can also be brought on by illnesses such Parkinson's disease or the medicines used to treat them.

A woman named Michelle experienced this firsthand. She had been diagnosed with Parkinson's disease. One evening she and her husband were driving home with their seven-year-old granddaughter named Amy. Michelle turned around in the car to look at Amy and saw someone sitting in the seat next to her. She was shocked and told her husband, "Stop the car, someone is in the back with Amy."[36] Her husband looked, but no one was there. He was able to convince Michelle that she was hallucinating that day, but she continued seeing things. Once she thought she saw someone walking around her house. Eventually, her doctors changed her medications and the hallucinations stopped.

Environmental toxins such as carbon monoxide or radon gas can also cause hallucinations. Even mold can cause people to see things that are not there. Mold likes warm, moist places and can be found just about anywhere it finds these conditions—including homes, cars, and schools. Many molds contain harmful compounds called mycotoxins. Prolonged exposure to mycotoxins can bring on psychosis, a mental condition that can include hallucinations.

Environmental engineer Shane Rogers frequently found mold in places he investigated that were thought to be haunted. According to Rogers, "There is definitely a significant difference between mold presence in haunted places versus not-haunted places. We have roughly five to six times more mold spores showing up in places that are reported haunted."[37]

Psychological Explanations

There may also be psychological explanations for the belief in ghosts. Psychology professor Chris French maintains that suggestibility can cause supposed ghost sightings. He says that when people are told they are going to experience something unusual, they are more likely to do so. French notes, "If you're shown around an old building and somebody says it's haunted, you'll notice every little creak and change in temperature in a way you wouldn't have done otherwise."[38]

> "If you're shown around an old building and somebody says it's haunted, you'll notice every little creak and change in temperature in a way you wouldn't have done otherwise."[38]
>
> —Chris French, head of the Anomalistic Psychology Research Unit at the University of London

Ghost sightings might also originate when people try to protect themselves emotionally from death. The thought of death being final can be very scary, and believing in life after death can soothe these fears. Visits from deceased loved ones provide some people with proof of an afterlife. As Hupp says, "There's still so much to this universe that we don't understand, and it's comforting to fill in the void with explanations. Supernatural explanations are often stated

Albert Einstein and the Dead

Some people believe that Albert Einstein's work is evidence that ghosts are real. They cite his first law of thermodynamics that says that energy cannot be created or destroyed; it simply changes form.

For example, when adding ice to a glass of warm soda, the cube will melt, but the soda will become colder. The amount of heat energy in the system (the glass with ice and soda) has remained the same, but the matter has changed form.

The human body is also a system of energy. It takes energy from food and changes it into kinetic energy (the energy of motion). The body also generates electrical energy through internal chemical reactions. Believers reason that, according to the first law of thermodynamics, the energy in a human body must go somewhere when a person dies. They argue that it is transformed into spiritual energy.

But physics has a different answer. It says that the energy in a human body goes into the environment when the body dies, just like that of all other organisms. Energy from the body is released as heat. Any remaining energy is transferred to bacteria or other creatures that consume a decomposing body.

---

with confidence, even when there's no actual evidence, and this confidence provides a false sense of actual truth."[39]

There are also phenomena called bereavement hallucinations, which psychologists describe as a reaction to acute grief. These hallucinations range from sensing a loved one's presence to feeling their touch to seeing them. According to author Karen Stollznow, "Various studies show that a staggering 30–50% of people have these experiences after someone has died. In fact, grief hallucinations are so common and benign that they are considered a normal part of bereavement. They are found across cultures, beliefs, and time, and they play an important part in the grieving and healing process."[40]

What Science Might Not Yet Know

Scientists contend that if ghosts were real, there would be hard evidence of their existence. So far, none has been found. Yet many people are steadfast in their beliefs that they have experienced something supernatural. They point out that science is making new discoveries every day. As neuroscientist Jeff Tarrant remarks, "So many things we once thought were magical or impossible—from magnets to medical cures—were simply mysteries awaiting a scientific explanation."[41] Believers wonder whether science simply has not figured out the properties of supernatural visits. Perhaps, they say, there are things that science still does not know.

Introduction: The Enduring Fascination with Ghostly Encounters

1. Quoted in Sarah Lemire, "16 Very Real Ghost Stories That'll Chill You to the Bone," *Today*, August 18, 2022. www.today.com.
2. Quoted in Lemire, "16 Very Real Ghost Stories That'll Chill You to the Bone."

Chapter One: What Are Ghosts, and Why Do They Appear?

3. Kerrie Erwin, "Why Some Souls Remain Earthbound—and How to Identify Their Presence," *Llewellyn Journal*, April 3, 2023. www.llewellyn.com.
4. Quoted in Lemire, "16 Very Real Ghost Stories That'll Chill You to the Bone."
5. Quoted in *The Night Owl*, "Campfire 13: A Psychic Journey," February 26, 2024. www.thenightowlpodcast.com.
6. Quoted in Bill Guggenheim.com, "About Bill Guggenheim," 2021. www.billguggenheim.com.
7. Quoted in Bill Guggenheim.com, "About Bill Guggenheim."
8. Quoted in John Blake, "Do Loved Ones Bid Farewell from Beyond the Grave?," CNN, September 23, 2011. www.cnn.com.
9. Karen Noe, "Your Deceased Loved Ones Are Okay and Want You to Know That," Open to Hope, May 13, 2023. www.opentohope.com.
10. Quoted in Laura Parnaby, "Colorado Teacher Eilish Poe, 25, Claims She Sees Ghosts After Miraculously Surviving Vicious Stabbing by Ex-Boyfriend Who Hid in a Crawl Space at Her House for 26 Hours Before Attack," *Daily Mail* (London), August 13, 2023. www.dailymail.co.uk.
11. Quoted in Parnaby, "Colorado Teacher Eilish Poe, 25, Claims She Sees Ghosts After Miraculously Surviving Vicious Stabbing by Ex-Boyfriend Who Hid in a Crawl Space at Her House for 26 Hours Before Attack."
12. Tanya Carroll Richardson, "Six Types of Spirit Guides and How to Communicate with Them," Mindbodygreen, March 27, 2021. ww.mindbodygreen.com.
13. Quoted in Ivory LaNoue, *True Stories of Angel Encounters*, YouTube, 2022. www.youtube.com/watch?v=GGnqXSt3wW8.
14. Quoted in Christine Rousselle, "'Angels, Demons, Spirits, and Souls Do Exist,' Says Exorcist Priest Who Warns Against Ouija Board Use," Fox News, October 30, 2023. https://www.foxnews.com.
15. Quoted in *True Scary Story*, "Behind the Rocking Chair," March 8, 2023. https://truescarystory.com.

Chapter Two: Making Themselves Known

16. Quoted in Veenu Sandal, "Mystery Behind Ghost Visits in Your Dreams," *Sunday Guardian* (New Delhi), January 19, 2019. https://sundayguardianlive.com.
17. Quoted in *Uncanny*, "The Blue Man," Series 3, Case 1, September 27, 2023.
18. Quoted in *Uncanny*, "The Blue Man."
19. Quoted in *Uncanny*, "The Blue Man."
20. Amy Bruni, *Ghost Hunting 101: Class 1*, YouTube, 2023. www.youtube.com/watch?v=pQ1IbLOQ2bY.

21. Quoted in *Astonishing Legends*, "The Hitchhiker of Mogollon Rim," October 28, 2023. https://astonishinglegends.com.
22. Quoted in Hana the Suburban Witch, *Demons and Negative Entities with Michelle Belanger—Witch Talks Podcast*, YouTube, 2024. www.youtube.com/watch?v=8Pry_7TBCog.

Chapter Three: How Do They Do It?
23. Jeff Tarrant, "As a Scientist, I Didn't Believe in Psychic Powers. Then I Experienced Something That Changed My Life," HuffPost, February 6, 2024. www.huffpost.com.
24. Quoted in *Uncanny*, "Dad's Phone," Series 4, Case 2, May 7, 2024.
25. Quoted in Maureen Kyle, "Mary Ann the Ghost Whisperer Says This Halloween Is Extra Spooky," WKYC Studios, October 29, 2020. www.wkyc.com.
26. Quoted in Hamza the Historian, *The Djinn & Dreams—Rosemary Ellen Guiley*, YouTube, 2021. www.youtube.com/watch?v=pbHRNZCs05c&t=5719s.
27. Quoted in LMN, *Ghosts Travel Through Portals in Woman's House (Season 2)—My Ghost Story*, YouTube, 2023. www.youtube.com/watch?v=8Fn-OzbFscY.
28. Quoted in Rousselle, "'Angels, Demons, Spirits and Souls Do Exist,' Says Exorcist Priest Who Warns Against Ouija Board Use."
29. Hana the Suburban Witch, *Demons and Negative Entities with Michelle Belanger—Witch Talks Podcast*.

Chapter Four: Ghosts of Many Cultures
30. National Park Service, *A Lingering Love*, June 5, 2015. https://npshistory.com.
31. Quoted in Frameglasseye, "The Flying Head," Reddit. www.reddit.com.
32. Quoted in *Astonishing Legends*, "The Elusive Force: A Powerful Polish Poltergeist, Part 1," April 13, 2024. https://astonishinglegends.com.

Chapter Five: Science Explains Ghosts
33. Quoted in Ayla Smith, "Well, We Regret Asking About Sleep Paralysis After Reading All of Your Responses About It," BuzzFeed, October 10, 2023. www.buzzfeed.com.
34. Quoted in Kenneth Biddle, "Investigating Artifacts at the Archive of the Afterlife," *Skeptical Inquirer*, April 22, 2020. https://web.archive.org.
35. Quoted in Benjamin Radford, "Are Ghosts Real?," LiveScience, October 6, 2023. www.livescience.com.
36. Quoted in Your Magazine, "Seeing Things: Michelle's Experience of Hallucinations." www.parkinsons.org.uk.
37. Quoted in Kate Golembiewski, "Are 'Paranormal' Experiences Due to Infrasound, Gas Leaks, and Toxic Mold?," Big Think, November 11, 2023. https://bigthink.com.
38. Quoted in Samuel Spencer, "The Science Behind Seeing Ghosts," BBC, August 14, 2023. www.bbc.co.uk.
39. Quoted in Radford, "Are Ghosts Real?"
40. Karen Stollznow, "Grief Hallucinations: Why We Sometimes See the Ghost of a Deceased Loved One," *Speaking in Tongues* (blog), *Psychology Today*, November 30, 2023. www.psychologytoday.com.
41. Tarrant, "As a Scientist, I Didn't Believe in Psychic Powers."

FOR FURTHER RESEARCH

Books

Adam Berry, *Goodbye Hello*. New York: Regalo, 2023.

Steve Gonsalves, *A Life with Ghosts*. New York: Gallery, 2023.

Michael A. Kozlowski, *American Ghost Stories: True Tales from All 50 States*. Canton, MI: Visible Ink, 2023.

J.R. Meza, *Your Haunted Brain: The Essential Guide to Understanding the Interplay Between the Science, the Psychology, and the Superstition of Ghost Hunting and Human Fear*. Self-published, Amazon Digital Services, 2024. Kindle edition.

Internet Sources

Tim Brown, "We Asked AI, 'Do Ghosts Exist?,'" Ghost Stop, February 20, 2023. www.ghoststop.com.

H. Addington Bruce, *Historic Ghosts and Ghost Hunters*. Project Gutenberg, 2009. First published in 1908 by Moffat (New York). www.gutenberg.org.

The Conversation, "Necromancers, Demons and Friendly Ghosts: Humans Have Been Fascinated with the Afterlife Since Ancient Mesopotamia," October 29, 2023. https://theconversation.com.

Hal Herzog, "Why Someone Might See the Ghost of a Pet," *Animals and Us* (blog), *Psychology Today*, April 10, 2024. www.psychologytoday.com.

Sarah Lemire, "Are Ghosts Real? What to Know About Hauntings and Paranormal Activity," *Today*, September 25, 2023. www.today.com.

Barry Markovsky, "Are Ghosts Real? A Social Psychologist Examines the Evidence," University of South Carolina, October 25, 2023. https://sc.edu/uofsc.

Sandra Martinez, "25 Common Signs from Deceased Pets," *Animal Communication* (blog), February 11, 2023. www.sandramartinez.co.uk.

Lisa Stardust, "10 Signs Your House Is Haunted (and What to Do About It)," *Teen Vogue*, October 17, 2023. www.teenvogue.com.

Websites

Association for the Scientific Study of Anomalous Phenomena
www.assap.ac.uk
This association is dedicated to scientifically investigating strange happenings. Its website contains reports on investigative findings as well as articles on several paranormal topics, including orbs, hauntings, and classic cases. It also offers readers a chance to request an investigation of a particular case.

Connect Paranormal
www.connectparanormal.com
This website links users to videos about ghosts and other paranormal topics. A few of the current videos on the site are *Haunted Alcatraz*, *Beyond the Scream*, and *Methods for Dealing with Dangerous Ghosts*.

Higgypop.com
www.higgypop.com
This website reports daily news about paranormal topics. It also includes in-depth articles about the supernatural world. Subsections include television and documentary reviews, ghost-hunting advice, and paranormal games.

How Ghosts Work
https://science.howstuffworks.com/science-vs-myth/afterlife/ghost.htm
An informative and thorough website that explores the beliefs and the science of topics such as EVPs, infrasound, and haunted houses.

The Shadowlands
https://theshadowlands.net
This website is a repository of over sixteen thousand true ghost stories, a state-by-state guide to haunted places, EVPs, an archive of photos and videos, and much more.

Skeptical Inquirer
https://skepticalinquirer.org
This is the website of a bimonthly magazine published by the Committee for Skeptical Inquiry, an organization that investigates extraordinary claims. A search for ghosts, hauntings, psychics, or similar topics on this site will bring up free articles that take a skeptical view of paranormal claims about these topics.

Your Ghost Stories
www.yourghoststories.com
This website provides experiencers with a place to share their paranormal encounters. It has a large collection of accounts written by readers as well as ghost pictures and videos. It also includes articles about ghosts and famous hauntings.

INDEX

Note: Boldface page numbers indicate illustrations.

after-death communication (ADC)
  inviting
    ghost hunting, 34–35
    Ouija boards and, 35, **35**, 36
    séances, 34
  messages during, 9–11
  public opinion about, 4
  during sleep, 15, 18–20, **20**
  "spirit phone" of Edison, 50
  term for, 10–11
  timing of, 11–13, **13**, 14
airplanes, 34
Albania, 40
American Ghost Stories (Kozlowski), 38–39
apophenia, 51–53
Arab cultures, 40

Baland Jalal, 50–51
banshees, 39–40
Belanger, Michelle, 14, 26, 35–36
bereavement hallucinations, 55
Berry, Adam, 31
Biddle, Kenny, 46–47, 52–53
Bienvenue, Justin, 32
Brisbine, Lindsey, 21–22
Broad, Claire, 11
Bruni, Amy, 24
Burgess, Forrest, 43
Burkett, Alyssa, 12–13

calveras, 43
carbon monoxide, 54
Chilling Podcast, The, 21–22
Christianity, demons in, 14–15
Chumacero, Sarah, 24
Churchill, Winston, 25
communication between living and dead. *See* after-death communication (ADC)
Coolidge, Grace, 25
crime-solving ghosts, 15

Day of the Dead, 43
Dellis, Brian, 33–34
demons, **16**
  basic facts about, 14
  encounter with, 15–16
  forms taken by, 26–27
  Ouija boards and, 35
  religious beliefs about, 14–15
  as "shadow people," 22–23
DiFrancesco, Ron, 12
Dinwiddie, William Walter, 50
Drake, Linda, 33

Edison, Thomas, 50
Einstein, Albert, 55
electrical equipment, as energy source for ghosts, 29–30
electromagnetic fields (EMFs), 47, **47**
electronic voice phenomena (EVPs), 31, 51–53, **52**
energy sources for ghosts
  electrical equipment, 29–30
  emotional energy of young people, 43
  first law of thermodynamics and, 55
  living being's energy, 30–31
  sound recording devices, 31
environmental toxins and hallucinations, 54
Erwin, Kerrie, 8–9, 14, 28–29, 30

Fiji, 40

flying heads, 40–41, **41**
Fox sisters, 48, **49**
Frazier, Karen, 20–21
French, Chris, 54

Gajewski, Joasia, 43–44
Gatollari, Mustafa, 49–50
Geismann, Suzanne, 20
Gettysburg, Pennsylvania, battlefield, 21
ghost hunters
   equipment of, 29–30, 31, 34–35
   as hoaxers, 48–50
ghosts
   as earthbound spirits, 9
   forms taken by
      flying heads, 40–41, **41**
      morphing figures, 27
      orbs, 20–22, **22**
      real people, 24–25
      "shadow people," 22–23
   general beliefs about, 8
   individual's openness to psychic connections and, 28–29
   percentage of American adults visited by, 11
   public opinion about, 4, 6, **7**
   types of
      banshees, 39–40
      crime-solving, 15
      helpful, 12, 14, 34, 38–39
      night hags, 40
      poltergeists, 43–45, **44**
      Pontianak, 42
      residual, 31–33
      trick-playing ghosts, 16–17, 45
      See also demons
ghost tours, 7
Grace, Elle, 36
grief hallucinations, 55
Guggenheim, Bill, 10–11
Guiley, Rosemary Ellen, 33

hallucinations, 53–54, 55
hauntings, residual, 31–35, **32**

Hayes, Derek, 6
hoaxers and hoaxes, 48–50, **49**
Hollis, Heidi, 23
Hupp, Stephen, 53, 54–55

imaginary friends, 21
Ireland, 39–40
Iroquois Indians, flying head of, 40–41

Japan, 40

Kahn, Nina, 18
kanashibari (night hag), 40
kana tevoro (night hag), 40
Kielty, Matt, 48
King, Stephen, 32–33
Kozlowski, Michael A., 38–39
Krasue of Thailand, 41

LaNoue, Ivory, 14
La Pavura Blanca, 37–39, **38**
Lincoln, Abraham, 25
Livon, Jodi, 16
Loft, Robert, 34
Luna, Hernando de, 37
Lynn, Loretta, 29, **29**

Malay culture, *penanggalan* of, 41, **41**
medications causing hallucinations, 54
Mexicans, 43
Mokthi (night hag), 40
molds, 54
Monsters Among Us (podcast), 39–40
morphing figures, 27
Mrs. Moon, 36
mycotoxins, 54

Native Americans, 37–39, **38**, 40–41
night hags, 40
nightmare, origin of word, 40
Noe, Karen, 11

orbs, 20–22, **22**
"Orbs and Shadows with the Light Witch" (*The Chilling Podcast* episode), 21–22
Otherworld (podcast), 27
Ouija boards, 35, **35**, 36

pareidolia, 53
Pavla Blanca, 37–39, **38**
penanggalan, 41, **41**
photographs
   images seen in mirrors in, 33–34
   orbs and, 21, 22
physics and ghosts, 46
planchettes, 35
podcasts about ghosts
   Burgess and, 43
   Chilling, The, 21–22
   Hayes and, 6
   increase in, 7
   Monsters Among Us, 39–40
   Otherworld, 27
Poe, Eilish, 12–13
poltergeists, 43–45, **44**
Pontianak, 42
popular culture, ghosts in, 6–7
portals, 33–34
psychic connections, ghosts and individual's openness to, 28–29
public opinion about ghosts, 4, 6, **7**

radon gas, 54
rapid eye movement (REM) sleep, 50–51
Reehil, Dan, 15, 35
reflections, 46–47
Reith, Anne, 18
Repo, Donald, 34
residual hauntings, 31–35, **32**
Richardson, Tanya Carroll, 14
Rogers, Shane, 54
Roosevelt, Eleanor, 25
Roosevelt, Theodore, 25

Samper, Jordyn, 51

Schrader, Dave, 18–19
scientific explanations for ghostly phenomena
   bereavement/grief hallucinations, 55
   electromagnetic fields, 47, **47**
   emotional self-protection from death, 54–55
   environmental toxins causing hallucinations, 54
   EVPs, 31, 51–53, **52**
   hoaxers, 48
   medications causing hallucinations, 53
   power of suggestion, 54
   real-life physical causes, 46
   reflections, 46–47
   sleep paralysis, 50–51
séances, 34
"shadow people," 22–23
Shining, The (King), 32–33
Showery, Allan, 15
Southeast Asia, ghosts of, **41**, 41–42
Stanley Hotel (Estes Park, Colorado), **32**, 32–33
Stollznow, Karen, 55
suggestibility, 54

Tarrant, Jeff, 28, 56
Thailand, 41
thermodynamics, first law of, 55
"third man factor," 12
trick-playing ghosts, 16–17

white lady, 37–39, **38**
White Sands National Monument, 37, 38
Wilder, Annie, 33
Wilhelmina (queen of Netherlands), 25
Winkowski, Mary Ann, 21, 30–31
World Trade Center on September 11, 2001, 12
Wyandot Indians, flying head of, 40–41

Cover: Fer Gregory/Shutterstock

4: Maury Aaseng
7: Aleksei Isachenko/Shutterstock
10: Nomad_Soul/Shutterstock
13: Michael O'Keene/Shutterstock
16: kittirat roekburi/Shutterstock
20: fast-stock/Shutterstock
22: ohenze/Shutterstock
26: gwoeii/Shutterstock
29: s_bukly/Shutterstock
32: Gwenn Taylor/Shutterstock
35: KinoMasterskaya/Shutterstock
38: Lario Tus/Shutterstock
41: Pictures From History/Newscom
44: Fizkes/Shutterstock
47: shutting/Shutterstock
49: Chroma Collection/Alamy Stock Photo
52: KinoMasterskaya/Shutterstock

ABOUT THE AUTHOR

Doreen Staskal makes her home in Colorado. She enjoys eating peanut butter sandwiches next to cold alpine lakes and searching for Columbine on high mountain trails. Her grandchildren keep her laughing, and she is working to improve her Candyland strategies.